Contents

What is a hurricane?

Hurricanes are big spinning storms. They start over the sea in tropical areas.

Near the equator, the sea is warm. Warm air above the sea rises up. More air from nearby gets sucked in. Big clouds form and start to spin.

The centre of the hurricane is called the eye. The eye is the calm spot. But around the eye, the winds are very strong, clouds are thick and rain is heavy.

eye

9

Every hurricane has a name. This makes it easier to track each one. Hurricane Irma hit Florida in the United States in 2017.

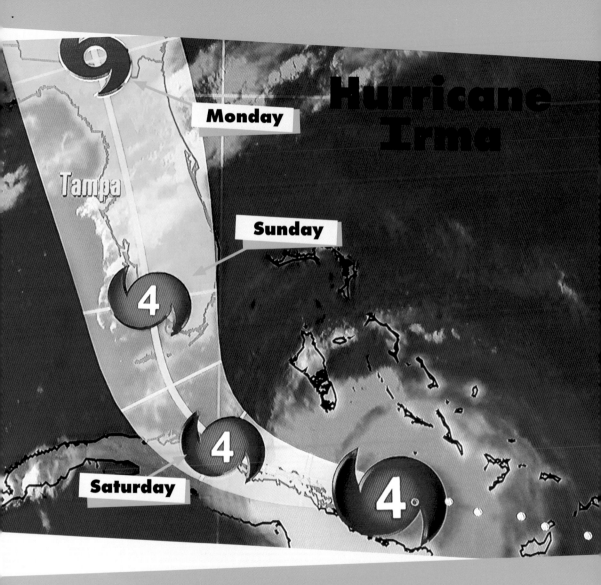

Tracking map of Hurricane Irma

11

When hurricanes get to the land, they can cause lots of damage. Palm trees bend in the wind. Buildings can be damaged.

palm trees

Huge waves hit the shore.
Water floods over roads and
into houses.

Strong winds blow.

They can even rip trees

out of the ground.

Staying safe

If people know a storm is coming, they can get ready. They cover windows with wooden boards to protect the glass.

Experts watch for storms. They tell people when to get to safety. People leave their homes. They can come back when the hurricane is over.

Glossary

calm quiet and peaceful

expert a person with great skill or who knows a lot about something

eye the calm area at the centre of a hurricane

hurricane a strong, swirling wind and rainstorm that starts over the sea

shore the place where the sea meets land

storm very bad weather; hurricanes, tornadoes and blizzards are types of storms

tropical the hot and wet areas near the equator

Find out more

How the Weather Works (How it Works), Christiane Dorion (Templar, 2011)

See Inside Weather and Climate (Usborne Flap Books), Katie Daynes (Usborne, 2014)

Thunder and Lightning (Weather Wise), Helen Cox Cannons (Raintree, 2014)

Websites

Discover information about lots of different types of weather, including extreme weather here:
www.metoffice.gov.uk/weather/learn-about/weather/weather-for-kids

For more facts, including how to tell the clouds apart, visit this website:
www.theschoolrun.com/homework-help/weather.

Comprehension questions

1. Where do hurricanes form?

2. What is the middle of a hurricane called?

3. How can people stay safe during a hurricane?

Index